CW00694651

HOUSE *of* BREAD

POEMS AND PAINTINGS FROM A PRAYER JOURNAL

BRUCE DRIVER

ryelands

For Barbara

First published in Great Britain in 2015

British Library Cataloguing-in-Publication Data
A CIP record for this title is available from the British Library

ISBN 978 1 906551 41 4

RYELANDS
Halsgrove House, Ryelands Business Park,
Bagley Road, Wellington, Somerset TA21 9PZ
Tel: 01823 653777   Fax: 01823 216796
email: sales@halsgrove.com

Part of the Halsgrove group of companies.
Information on all Halsgrove titles is
available at: www.halsgrove.com

Printed in China by the Everbest Printing Co Ltd

House of Bread

The Basic. Food of Life.
To call a city that?
Jewish wisdom, Hebrew language
Are one.
Bethlehem means House of Bread.
Christmas Crib of earliest memory.
My identity revealed there. Returning
Now provokes neither shrug nor apology.
Genesis, beginning, yeast: Bethlehem.
Crib in the House of Bread.

It's no child's plaything I see. This pivot
Of history's meaning where soldiers come,
Shepherds, poets, kings.
And those with obscure and pitiful longings
For a better life.
People like me.

Christ born in the House of Bread.
Readily we meet him in
Midnight Mass.
At any Mass.
Bethlehem boy, he learned to turn
Himself into Bread.

Feeding on that Bread turns us
Into him.
Promise.
Bethlehem.
We are a House of Bread.

Foreword

This is a book of mystery, devotion and enchantment. The author, Fr. Bruce, is elderly now, living with his wife in a college for retired priests in East London, close to his beloved Thames. For many years he has been compiling what he calls his 'Prayer Journal': short poems interleaved with watercolour paintings, for which he has an uncommon flair.

Enigmatically he has called it 'House of Bread'. What can this mean? The 'bread of heaven' perhaps, though that would be aiming high and few would venture to call a house after it? The 'daily bread', for which Jesus bids us pray? Or the bread of the Eucharist which plays so large a part in Fr. Bruce's spirituality? But that would imply an ecclesiastical setting which is far from what he has in mind. What matters is that these poems sit well within the tradition of mystical verse in which English poets have excelled for the last seven hundred years.

And the paintings in watercolour – of many subjects and in many places, but best perhaps when related to London's waterways – also have an enchanted quality that grows upon one as one knows them better.

This is a book to take in short steps, though there is nothing wrong in reading it from cover to start with. As the author says: 'choose the words or images that strike you. Return to them frequently and don't rush'. Do this and you will be richly rewarded.

Sir Hugh Beach

Introduction

Brother Giles SSF first pointed out that poems and watercolour paintings had become the means for me of keeping a Prayer Journal. My own part of the Community (Third Order, Society of St Francis), through its Study and Prayer Enabling Group, became enthusiastic about publishing some of the Journal's content. Sir Hugh Beach and Denise Mumford took an active and effective part in enabling this to happen. Simon Butler at Halsgrove Publishing has been very helpful and supportive. I am more than grateful to them all for their encouragement.

You are being invited to look over my shoulder at my decades-long attempt to be open to the Mystery of God, which is how I understand prayer.

Bruce Driver TSSF
Eastertide 2015

A Priest's Life

Old Priest

Gathering dust.
Still long enough for all
To settle round him.
Hopes, cries, the things
Told twice.
Ageing hand on a crucifix
Collects these for
One beyond time.

Near the Sacrament

Half-light, passing vehicles
Murmur to the dark.
Candlelight.
Holy Sacrament Chapel.
Morning Prayer within
A hand's breadth of
The Body and Blood of Christ.
Watchman before the King of kings,
Who is guarding whom
In this perfect place
As a day begins?

2013

Morning Prayer

Flustered, asthmatic,
Blown into the Chapel.
Her chatter breaks the silence.
Without resentment we settle again.
Slowing our struggle for air
To a timeless rhythm,
Calming, healing.
Leaving aside our breathing,
For God's.

Evening Prayer

I come wearied, to sit with God.
Thursday, piano notes slipping
From the Hall. Dancing Class.
Occasionally Music Hall,
More often Degas' Rehearsal Room,
Tutus in pastel.
Ballerinas' liquid stretching.
Pouring myself out, laying my
Nothing before God. Is this
Movement of soul dance?
Elegant, as music for ballet,
Or funny, Music Hall's pathos?
Prayer's restoration.
Poise, and Laughter.

The Ark

Tuesday evening Mass,
Accompanied by dog-training
In the Hall.
An occasional choir, inspiring
Devotions.
Just before Mass, Rachel brings
Her Mum and her Noah's Ark.
I admire her carefully coloured
Animals. A dog's voice rises.
We turn marvelling, to Mass.

Dancers

Light on water;
God dances.
A priest casts a lifetime's words
Carefully into the light.
They dance.
Unnoticed, unconsidered.
Except by a child.

Attention

All is gift; undeserved.
In the silent satisfying waiting
Notice what is withheld,
Not yet given;
Even attention.
No anxiety intrudes,
No longing for solution.
No confusion of distracting and
Threadbare puzzles,
With mystery.

Annunciation

A day declares itself,
Offering its first gift.
Water; clean in shower and glass.
How to respond?
An astonished 'yes' in that
Silent waiting which holds.
Until the moment when
Heaven and earth are first
Marked in measured signing
With the Cross.
The breaking of long silence; a
Day's first words:
'In the name of the Father and of the Son
And of the Holy Spirit'.
This day's intention;
Complete as it may be.

Water

Quarrel with God.
Another test for Him against man's
Mind?
Meribah and Massah, said
The Exodus Jews.
Rock in a wilderness, like man's
Intransigence.
Water there, of God's choosing.

Man is two thirds H20.
Life is told in water, unremembered
Till there is desert; or flood.
Jesus knew Himself as wellspring,
A few drops fall from the hand of
A priest heralding
Someone's second birth.

The passing years, Christening
Upon Christening.
Old priest's trembling hand; stronger
Moment by moment his holy fear.
Another child's destiny.

Versicle and Response

Is God?

Bird sings.
Give it your attention.

Turning aside

Who are you?
Who am I?
I am one under a tree
Who waits,
Wiping the world's
Fevered brow.

At Table

I hear voices claiming places;
'He is senior'. And,
Aware only of a sense of
Being out of place, notice
These attempts at recognition
Spoil the feast.
Better be the old dog collecting
Scraps; sacrament beneath clamour
And the starched linen.
Seen, and at once forgotten.

Bruce Dunit
2014.

Veteran

Exchanging ordination dates
With a young priest:
'You are a veteran'.
Less is known
Than at the beginning.
Yet the gift of sitting still
Brings pilgrims
Grasping their prayers.
Whetting them on an old stone
Considered untrained
In his weathering.
Living more deeply by a little,
I offer my nothing;
Left only with my prayers and
A sufficiency of joy.

At the door

Crow. Crow!
Voice; all voice.
Throwing a dark cloak
Over the morning's shoulders.

Three Monk Poems

It happens;
The coming of Light.
Scientist, this predicted and long known,
Looks elsewhere.
Monk rises to witness Light's coming.
Awed by this gift;
Moved to a lifetime's watching.
Light; man's predecessor,
Known to Scientist and Monk.
Monk, alone before each day's dawning,
Is marked by change.
Patient watcher reaching beyond time;
Shaped by Light's soundless word.

Cherishing words
Carved by silences.
Holding one word in the heart
Until all its echoes
Have become still water,
At rest in the depths.

Birds' voices are leaves dancing.
Crow, all rock and mineral,
Celebrates earth's core.
And I? I, dawn's dew-web voice,
Gather light threads for
Another day's cloth.

Prayer Beads

Jesus Prayer

Movement of God's
Compassionate memory,
Around a circle of beads
Touches my failing
Life in its letting go. And
Blesses those long spaces
People once occupied.
'Κύριε Ἰησοῦ Χριστέ, *
Υἱὲ τοῦ Θεοῦ, ἐλέησόν
με τὸν ἁμαρτωλόν'
Sparse words recalled and
Stumbled over without anxiety.
God offers the Prayer.

Beadsman

It's never been said
Since I've been here,
Among these 17th century
Cloisters.
Beadsman;
A word unused.
Earlier than our Courts.
Old Saxons spoke it; 'Beda'; 'Prayer'.
Caught as an almsman, in
History's binding to benefactors.
Telling my beads.
Lost in counting for
Bishop John Warner**
And other Saints.

*Lord Jesus Christ, Son of God have mercy on me a sinner.

**Founder of Bromley College.

Living in the beads

Show me, Lord, how to
Live in my frailty;
Watching the beads
Become my cell;
And there teaching
Me everything.

Continuum

Silence extends the day through;
Prayer is without ceasing.
My bead cell is,
In its circling, quite still.

Companion

A few trees; worn,
Unsure; gathered along a
Station fence.
Seasons change;
I worship with these trees.
We watch together.
Silver birch vested in priestly white.
Bright for Nativity
Among winter's dark trees.
Sparkling in spring sunshine;
Resurrexit.
Faithful tree, ministering to my
Time's passing.
Agnus Dei before the clatter
Of a train.

Lament

My fellow worshippers
Have been taken.
Pogrom at the station.
Trees guard seasons
No more.
Silver birch cut down;
Priest and congregation.
Bare wire fences tell of
Other places of death.
And worse times.

Margaret

Is it confusion, or another mode
Of living
Beyond a mirror whose either side
Is bright and firm?
Passing through always muddles me.
Margaret's clear who I am,
Poor returning priest.
I know now, after all these years
That she is quite sure.
Only I am confused.
Holy bread yields to Margaret's
Commentary on something else.
Occasionally we find the Lord's Prayer
And a common voice.
Margaret is healed,
Transparent in the light of another
World beyond mine.
Somehow, I too will get better.

Song of God

Bhagavad Gita,
Song of God.
Faithful reciting
Scriptures;
Qu'ran, Gospel, Torah,
Sanatana dharma;
Eternal Law and
Divine Teaching revealed,
Shaping children and adults;
Zaddikim
Becoming God's song.

2013

Riddles

Silence so infinite that
Words once written
Slip beyond a page.
Unassuming, they offer a quiet
That does not deafen.

'Better Sorts of Precision'
(Rowan Williams)

Axiom.
All homilies should emerge from silence.
Better, actually be silent.
Let the Gospel shake the stillness
And return to it;
For time and half a time.
Common Worship, measured; and
The Ordinary of the Mass
Left to Tallis.
Nothing more.
No foolish hymn.
No fidgeting at heaven's curtain.

Priest

Used.
One whose passion is
Marked by the anger of
Life's battering; the
Touch of crowds at the
Hem of every moment.
A day's silences,
Born of long prayer,
Gather this harvest.
Awakening and joy bring
God's healing; and
Forgiveness.

Sufficiency

A wise priest knows
That he has nothing to offer
But presence.
No words; no half-digested fragments
Of others' expertise.
Silent presence.
It is enough.

2001

Seasons

Advent

Left by the sea on
This beach;
Until a later tide
Lifts me to stranger
Shores; where
Gulls question another
Moment of vocation.
Relic found among
Shingle,
And shards of ancient boats.

Epiphany

Journey to history's
Starlit moment.
Later these reticent Kings disappear unheard,
Into a private desert.
Here, a family remains
Floodlit for a lifetime.
Duty observed with courage and
Grace; admirable, its daily trudge.
Is too much placed on
Hereditary shoulders?
Five years offered is enough
In the light of one
Permanent star. Beyond are
Fields and quiet squares,
Retrieved from
Endless desert.

Prayer in Winter

Early morning birth of light.
Prayer loosed from shadows.
Light hugs dark, presenting
At its best.
An atmosphere delivered by
Visible breath
Among muttered Psalms.
Night's edge blurred by light.
This contrast felt, whilst
London's traffic fails to jostle
Silence.
Prayer escapes readily
And I am myself,
In Winter.

Winter in Essex

Cock crows
In this once a year dark.
Pleshey it must be, a
Third decade of Cell Retreats.
Three times was it cock; and
A significant telling?
Old cock falls into
Companionable silence.
Waiting, he and I;
One small bird sings the Hallowing.

2012.

In Choir

Cock is silent this morning.
Has death or bad temper intervened?
No Lauds today old feathered monk;
I am alone.
Cock is silent this morning.

Phos Hilarion*

Evening Prayer.
Country dark in Essex;
The Blessing of Light
Stirs imagination.
At dusk in London
Winter skies are full of human light.
Pleshey leaves no room
For fools' objections;
My God shall make
My darkness to be bright.

*Hail gladdening light

2013

Waiting at the Tomb

Laying the weight of suffering
Against heavy stone.
For unmeasured time
Nothing moves.
The stone rolls
Vast emptiness into sight.
Waiting becomes meaning,
And Presence.

Waiting at the Tomb II

The great stone;
Earth's circle,
Shutting death inside.
Our hopeless
Waiting, heavy with suffering.
Unexpected, unnoticed,
Earth's sudden rolling aside.
And God revealed within.

2012.

Hidden Shoals

No fishing boats,
Only the cries of children.
Suddenly the sky
Is full of gulls.
A moment's emptying
And there remain now
Quite alone,
Children and the sea

Rain at Night

Rain sings,
Touching some hidden
Note of meaning.
All is deeper than sleep
Which intrudes
On a night's wakefulness.
Carelessly shrugging
Prayer aside.

Angel of the Tides

Meeting on a childhood beach;
I saw then that something of me
Left with each tide.
I knew that one day, on an ebbing tide
I would go with the angel.
A monk's work; waiting in a lifetime's
Quiet for that end.
Content with silence, I hear the surf.
And the angel's voice.

Lawns and Singing Trees
(Song of Songs 8.13)

More here
Than haven for me;
Misfit in life's shirt.
More than
Litany of gardens;
Eden; Babylon; Gethsemane;
Resurrection; Kensington;
Chelsea Physic.
Here, given these
Lawns and
Singing trees,
My companions have
Three centuries
Listened for your voice.
And fifty years
More.
Let me hear it.

Harvest

They were here once
But now they're gone.
Rivers fallen from
London's pockets like
Whitsun toffees.
'Westbourne, Tyburn, Walbrook,
Effra, Fleet.'
'Bollo Brook, Counter's Creek.'
And all those Ditches;
'Parr, Cock and Pye, Carbunkle; Black.'
'Pudding Mill River.'
The English 'Moselle', under
White Hart Lane.
Some were covered;
Lost deliberately.
We're not sure where.
Rivers know; and, recalling their
Treatment, will one day surface.
Returning when
Seas rush the Estuary and
Old Thames gathers
His City.

London

The Wheel

London walking to work?
Unthinkable. The
Wheel is the rock on which
London stands.
And moves.
Jesus is not remembered
For wheels.
Sandals, hooves and boats
Fixed his pace; the
Steady, mindful steps
Necessary when
Setting one's face
Towards Jerusalem.

White Air

Air above a departing Tube,
Cold.
Morning draped in frost's light.
Winter's extravagance disguised
By breath.
Frozen stillness moving to birdsong.
Revelation.
White Air.

Listening

Song Thrush.
Psalmist's voice
In Canning Town.
Silence.
Absence?
Not in this waiting.
A moment's joy is full
Of singing;
In Canning Town

The Day; the Hour

South London's
Affectionate streets.
Small houses, like soldiers
Climbing hills.
Regular.
Those, once for toffs, and grander,
Scattered among dusty palms;
Paintwork dripping and peeled.
London tired; unresponsive to an
Unseeing eye.
Easily misjudged, underestimated.
London. Never prepared;
Always ready.

White Hart Lane

Childhood's steps along the
High Road.
Jellied eels by doors of pubs;
And the Game.
Fifty years. Turkish kebabs
Mark a walk from Seven Sisters.
But the Lane remains the Lane.
A ball still stays in touch with grass,
Even on the Jumbotron.
At the Lane.

Cool London

I, muffled in my
Dr Who scarf.
Ducks on Catford Pond's ice,
Standing confident
In their own colours.

Lenten Responsory
(Thomas Tallis c1505-85)

Returning from Mass.
Tallis's anthem spills, with me,
Across London.
Riverbus turns against the wash;
Movement surprises.
Tallis, like the old River,
Lives.

Poem Room
(After Dylan Thomas)

Scrap of paper on a knee
Does for my scribbling, praying day.
Parlour, if I had one, would
Remain parlour and
Cocoa safe from dipping pen.
If I had one.
'Real bards have poem rooms.'
Murmurs from Wales ruffle the Thames,
But not South London.

Superman

Above the River
This station opens doors on both banks.
From home, Wren took boat to St Paul's.
Suspended over the Thames
Blackfriars makes Superman of me.
In his skiff,
Wren knew otherwise.

At the Ballet

Dancing Trees.
Held in the glass of tall buildings.
Still in waiting silence.
Until frozen structures
Move to wind's orchestra.
The grace of the trees
Becomes a minuet. And
Tall buildings dance.

The Day After

All the movement
Is there;
And the stillness.
Feet on a London pavement; and the
Long east-west
Clatter of a Tube.
Monday.
The day after.
Wafer laid quietly
On a paten; soft
Voice of a priest.
Christ remembered;
Risen and ascended
Into bread.

Gatsby

"I want to go on
that spinning wheel".
Child's voice on a train,
Above the River and
The one great Eye.

Morning Suit

Lad keeping door at the
Strand Palace Hotel.
Top hat and
Shoes, too pointed,
Curling upwards.

Mislaid

Below Tower Bridge
Spray flies from the speeding
Riverbus.
London passes, painted by
Foam and flights of gulls;
Not seen by this boat's children,
Dull in their self-interest.
Noisy.
Asleep through another
Lost day.

2012.

Mottingham Sunday

Rag and bone man's
Horse and Cart
Passing St Edward's,
After Mass in SE9.
Another conflation of time by
Memory, poverty and
London's enduring joy.

Koinonia*

Clapton in summer;
East London on the Lea.
Among the cockneys and
The middle classes,
Hasidim and Burqas, in
London's easy air.

*Fellowship, communion

2014.

Pilgrimages

Godward

Pilgrim tested this
Journeying year;
Koya san, Freeland, Compostela;
Old traveller seeking
How to love the world and
Reject its idolatry;
Until pilgrimage settles;
Quiet under a College tree, and
Journeys from Morning to Evening Prayer,
One Mass to another.

Irreverent Journeys

A compulsion of travellers?
This people of an imperial past
And a wandering present.
What do Indonesians see in our
Arrivals from the air?
Endlessly in search of sun, sex,
All day music, and cool beer.
Is there respect?
Are we pilgrims. Mindful of
The eternity in an Indonesian eye.
Or trespassers.
Ignorant.
Believing, with brutal devil's contempt
That our money is sufficient offering.

Distances

Crossing horizons;
Above London,
Planes tell of long journeys.
Far places catalogued;
Pictures in another album.
I, seated here; not moving;
Still as may be.
Once more a day's inner journey begins.
Farthest horizons; distances
Unimagined.

Evangelists

Four windmills on a
Green Camino hill.
Grinding abandoned with
Ancient mills and the
Regret of history.
Energy harvested by
Slim giants;
Ghostly against
Spain's cobalt sky.

Ascent of a man

Age makes the skies larger,
Increasingly intimate.
My place among them
Becomes possible, more assured.
Only in silence and the
Looking up
Is this grace given;
My way opened, and
This first step taken.

Plains of Leon

Between place.
Destination not quite found.
Self always ahead,
Smudged on
Someone's horizon.

Life Vows

At first glance,
A Poor Clare.
Hair black, piled high and
White banded headphones
Say otherwise. Yet
I was convinced by
Noise I could see
In the girl's head;
And fear beneath.

Poem on August 6th

Am I light or dark,
Carrying, as I do,
My shadow;
Everywhere I go?
Seemingly unreal,
Insubstantial,
Until I trip over it.
Does it mark the
Earth as I pass;
Leave a stain.
Is my shadow
Burned into the surface?

Ninety ninth sheep
(Luke 15)

Or, perhaps
The prodigal hundredth.
Daily doses of grace
Find me once more
Shouldered by the
Story teller.
Pocketed as a coin.
Bleating.

2013.

Ancient Paths
(Jeremiah 6.16)

The ancient paths
Will not be dull,
For the one walking
Is fresh to them.
Brothers have tested the ways;
Time and long experience
Form the cloak now worn.
But all is new;
The walker faces his own horizons;
And must discover trust
In what is universally open.

Franciscan Meditations

Painting Our Lady

Crowing cock calls the day.
I wait.
The dark holds words peacefully.
Painting Our Lady.
I prepare for a day of days.
Silent waiting on light;
On God's gift.
When will I be ready?
Brush, pigment, paper, light;
God gives these.
Time cupped lovingly in God's hand
For that moment.
A poor man's first mark.

Learning Poverty

Blessed are the poor in spirit,
for theirs is the kingdom of heaven.
Matthew 5. 3

A poor man;
I have much.
One who knows poverty
Has nothing.
A poor man;
Dominant 'I' grasping;
Entombed Lazarus, still bound.
A lifetime's discipline;
Poverty has many teachers.
The prize: to have nothing,
Save a last cry of joy.

Antiphonal

In the light of the tree,
I find myself.
Old friends;
Soundless greeting.
Does the tree need me?
We bring ourselves, the
Tree and I.
Purity lies in that.
Together, we know joy.

Franciscan

Blessed are the poor in spirit,
for theirs is the kingdom of heaven.
Matthew 5. 3

Wearing one shirt,
Sitting before one
Plate of food.
The anticipated received as
Unexpected.
Surprised by gift;
One clean shirt, one plate of food;
One new day.
There is no desire for more.
Poverty in this
Not wanting?
Simplicity.
Abundance perceived.
Humility.
God's freedom.

Tabor

Air bubbles in a glass
Attract angled light.
Diamonds, suspended before
The seer.
At once,
Blinded to other images,
His days are fulfilled.

Prayer with Animals

Stranger in a son's house.
Cat; black, suspicious,
Eyes larger than herself;
Prepares to run.
Crow has followed me;
London voice,
Dark amid falling snow
And the singing of country birds.
We settle, Cat and I.
Content together in the
Silence.
And the waiting.

Testament

My Life;
Prayer and Listening.
Prayer: devotional Bible reading,
Office, Mass, and the
Long Silence.
Factory, home and hospice,
Pub, shop and street;
There I have listened.
Nothing much else,
My Life;
Nothing practical.
Except, every two days, the
Making of bread.
Remembered for bread?
Best forgotten.
Better, Jesus' way;
Remembered in bread.
The one useful thing
Of a lifetime. The
Making of bread.

2010

Stigmata

St Thomas' day,
Pre-occupied with
Markings.
Trust expressed bodily;
St Francis at La Verna.
Old faithful,
Souls wounded by
Cross bearing
Unseen and unseeing;
Kneel at some
Hidden altar.
Marked by God and man
For love's sake.

Old Trees
(after Ryokan)

"The old pines are
Full of poems." In
Blake's Peckham or
Ryokan's Japan; these are
Angels without disguise.
Trees singing with the
Voice of the sea.

Brother wind

At prayer before light,
Fresh; mobile;
Offering up high volume
Musical praise.
Our brother calls us with an
Insistent clarity to be
Present to God.

Putting on my Habit
(11 January 2014)

Being a Religious is
Marked today in
Community.
We've grown into
Our vows,
At least I have,
Across sixteen years of
Profession. The life's become
Habit worn daily.
Gathered by pilgrimage in
Wimbledon for
Celebrations with a
Promise; further
Journeys in the
Footsteps of St Francis.

Oyster Shell

Outside; weathered roof;
Tiles sloping, curved;
Old man turning to bone.
Inside: white, smooth;
Cool as love's touch.
Evolution's feminine grace;
Holder of the Life.

Creatures

One pure note,
Perfect hallowing.
Machine's complex
Engineering,
Calculation of the
Curve of light.
Man admires his skills.
Bird, unheard,
Is ignored.

2014

2013

Kiyomizu-dera

Traffic in a Holy city.
Still Kyoto's silence
Expands within; chanted by
Crow amidst
Buddhist shrines.

Promised

All land,
Every grain of earth, is
Holy.
Promised; full of promise.
One plant's
Mysterious cells in their thousands,
And stone's soundless voice
Crying gospel to the
Universe.

Balaam's Donkey
(Numbers 22)

Speaking little
On a lifetime's
Narrow paths.
My attempts to be faithful
Justly beaten by
The rod of time.

Bodkin

Obsolete word.
Unrecognised by many ears.
Overlooked herald of
Peace, and fulfilment of
Scripture's dream;
Weapon becoming
Domestic tool.
Dagger once; now a
Maker of holes in cloth,
Drawing threads
At a cottage hearth.

Via

The day's long cross-shaped
Pilgrimage; its wood heard
Dragging through my dust.
A dark shadow opening forward
Onto light.

Courage

We are always
A child taking
The first step;
Every day.
Until dying day.

Transitus

A peculiarly
Franciscan word;
Eve of St Francis' day;
Eve of renewal of vows.
Transitus; a
Passing over;
From death to life,
Old life to new.
A day's shared journey
Peculiarly one's own.

"A Thousand Hands After Just One Coin" (Han Shan)

And all the while
It's someone else's;
Perhaps the Emperor's
As Jesus demonstrated;
Or simply untouchable,
As St Francis insisted.
Forget coins,
It's better for hands
To seek other things,
As Han Shan suggested:
"Clap time for the
Flowers as they dance."

Feast of the Conception of Our Lady

'Heaven in Ordinary';
George Herbert's phrase
Wraps this day's significance
For my journey to
Balaam Street.
Pilgrimage to St Philip's, near
Forty years since
SDC* in its East London slum,
Caught my imagination.
And my prayers;
Making mentor of a Founder,
Father Andrew; his
Quiet Franciscan vocation
Sustaining mine.

*Society of the Divine Compassion

Summa Banana

Banana at the War's end;
Mythical almost to my
Skin-on first bite.
Affectionate later, our relationship;
And like all the material universe
Banana has become symbol of
Theological significance.
Eyeing my dog collar the
Young man in Sainsbury's,
Loading a rack of bananas, complained,
"I wish I was doing God's work";
As if feeding London being
God's work, had never occurred to him.
Generations of children in
School assemblies discovered otherwise;
The very young and those
Sophisticated 'A' level scientists.
Faced with a promise to see something
No human eye had ever seen;
My humble banana turned
Laughter into awed silence,
When slowly peeled to reveal the
Fruit itself, which, until that moment,
Had remained hidden in its unique
Created magnificence.

Fountain in Umbria

Silence in a suburban church;
Full of people listening
To water's song,
From a small fountain by the font.
Franciscans, not in the
Square at Assisi;
Their quiet in London
Blessed as if they were.
Stripped bare of everything
Except their closeness to
Francis and the Lord he served.

Tree Cathedral

I do not feel anger in a tree.
I do not feel anger in my tree.
Teach me good tree.
Is it your great arm
Reaching heavenward that heals?
Cell by cell we stand together
Looking upward.

2005.

On the Path to the Slip Gate

Listening to miniature daffodils
As I pass among them;
A human voice interrupts.
I am again, as always,
Disconnected.
How hard it is to be dragged
From deep communion to
Surface mind.

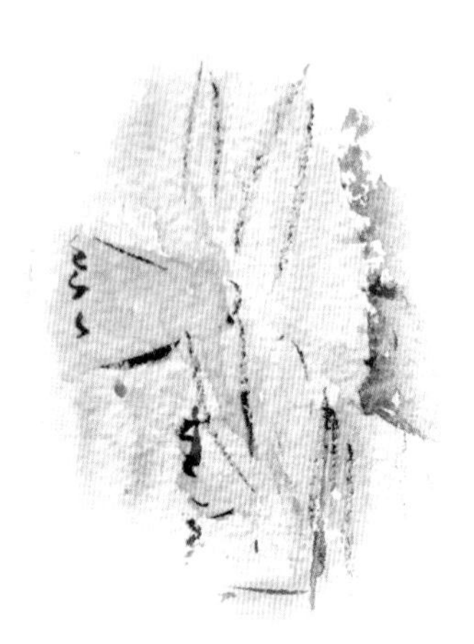

Jubilate

Bubbles singing in a glass;
God is never without praise.

HEAD
1999

‘The Joy which seizes my soul’
(Blessèd Angela of Foligno)

Can a dull Anglican; old,
Smothered in sceptics
Be seized?
Word of quality,
Volcanic, even in South London.
In the silence of the
Volcano’s heart
Truth comes from outside.
I am seized.

Twice Blessed

Christ’s unknowing mirrors,
Beggars in our streets.
The burden of His call is
Arresting, demanding and philosophical;
We dare not pass by.
St Francis gave to beggars when asked
‘In the name of God’.
Now it is the Franciscan giver who
Mentions God, in benediction.

Love's Interrogation

Ask a question.
We were taught that, endlessly.
No-one considered
Where this absolutism might lead;
How the demand for answers consumes;
Masking fears of silence; of no answer.
Beyond our tiny cries the
Steady voice of the Questioner,
But can we hear that
It is we who are being questioned.
"Who do you say I am?"

2013

Elixir 21
(after George Herbert, priest)

Is it possible to bound
A life satisfactorily;
And with an Office?
Reciting scripture before, and
After a day's labours?
Herbert believed so;
And so lived; with others.
The day, found measured,
Opened its paradoxical,
Poetic way to
Quiet purpose.
And lives with it.

Wilderness

Although necessity
Draws into conversation,
Silence is truer ground; when
Its distinctive voice calls;
Delay is no longer possible.

Thy Name

Holding troubled souls
In Light's perfection; an
Early Hallowing.

Lady Poverty

Only simplicity offers
Guidance to our poor steps
For any life; not least
In the muddle of public office.

2006

Transfiguration

Lenten waiting.
The Cross appears as great Opening.
The day gathers in the light.

At~one~ment

The great Opening of the Cross;
Causeway linking human and divine;
Atonement.

Memory

20th Century

The Dictators strode around
My birth into
An Age of Infamy.
What red is this that stains
My hands?
Blood shed that I might be.

Home Front

My pregnant mother
Tests barrage balloons, to put
Others' planes at risk;
Carrying me, complicit
Into the War effort.

ENDEAVOUR

Victorian Shadows on My Wall

Grandma's.
Kettle on an open fire,
Long handled forks
In the hearth. And
Bread for toasting,
Or dripping.
Looking after an old penny, and
Pounds taking care......

Pillars of Salt

Was that yesterday?
Everything was yesterday;
Even today.

Blades

Abstraction and analysis
Are dangerous tools.
You can cut your soul with them.

Confidere

Old man's
Confidence in God.
In manus tuas, Domine.
Confidere
Reflects as light off water
In love's gift
And acceptance. Oh the
Endless beauty of this dance;
And the holding, holding
Of each ruptured soul there,
Where the dance is
Still and yet is
Still the dance.

August 1940

Shirt sleeved,
Waistcoat open, an
Old man awaiting the
Drone of aircraft
Up the Estuary;
Hears only the
Slap of tides
Against a jetty.

Gentler Age

Voice.
Memorable among the Second World War's
'Day of infamy'; 'Finest hour'.
Voice at the end;
Girl in VE Day's celebrating crowd;
'I hate Hitler for what he made us do'.
Looking back.
Seeing forward; wise to
Blood's reckoning.
Judgement's voice.
Enormity of
God's Forgiveness.

73rd Anniversary

Did they know it was
The Feast of the Assumption of Our Lady,
That East End day in 1938?
Before the destruction
And the separation.
I remember his return in 1945,
And our meeting.
Shanklin's sea that summer was
Blue beyond blue, to
Another first sighting.
Onlooker at the remaking
Of a marriage.
Resting my scrap of paper on a copy of
'The Cloud of Unknowing.'

Berlin

Two cities becoming one;
Haunted still by
Terror.
Time is compressed,
What seemed long ago
Is only now considered.
A gloomy car park
Marches its ghosts
Above the Bunker.

Slummocking Feet

An old lady trudges;
Across the street, shuffling; scuffling.
'Pick up your slummocking feet!'
My mother's voice re-opens a
Century of marching.
Army cadet afternoons; the
Lift of heavy boots from grass
To the regular beat of a drum.
Signing for five rounds of
Live ammunition and the
Ease of target hitting.
I never thought then how
Simply a man might fall.
Five brass cases
Surrendered empty at the
School Range door.
'Pick up your slummocking feet!'
I was thirteen.

2014

St Oswald

King of Northumbria
Dying in battle this day
One thousand three hundred
And seventy two years past.
Amid our own wars
Truth is confessed,
Perhaps only to ourselves
And to God:
For some of us
Battles are normal;
Even as others pray for peace.
And we all lay
One blood red rose at the
Unknown soldier's tomb.

Old

Old is being:
Invisible;
Inconsequential; and
"In my way."

Last Woodsman

Six decades and still
Wood's smooth surface,
Under my plane then,
Satisfies; enduring, its clean,
Resinous smell.
An old man with adze and eye
Shapes oak coffins
Without measure or mark;
And takes that skill to his own grave.

Meetings

My father, my brother;
I can see them now,
At War's end and just after.
My father by the door
In khaki; a kit-bag,
His smile uncertain, like mine;
We'd never met before.
He was thirty,
Younger than my sons.
I was three and 'It' was over.
He was home.
Two springs later in a
Pram under our apple tree
I found Peter and we were four.
They're all gone now;
Mother, father, brother; and
Our meetings are indestructible
In the day's prayer-light.

Memorial

Forgotten; I am become
One who forgets.
Faces reel in
A long past;
Lost like my own.
Joy remains;
God remembers.

2014

The White Umbrella

Who's the girl with the
White umbrella I've
Painted in the
Paris rain?
Pygmalion of the
Brush, do I hope
We'll meet one day?
Yet painting what
I know tells me
This girl's promise is
Already given.
She brought me to life
With a long ago kiss;
Barbara and her white umbrella;
In the Paris rain.